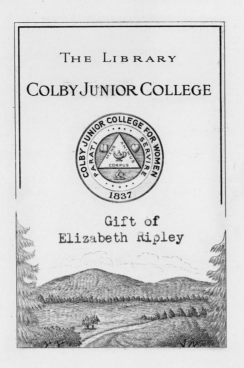

GOYA

GOYA

A Biography by
ELIZABETH RIPLEY

With Drawings, Etchings
and Paintings by Goya

NEW YORK   OXFORD UNIVERSITY PRESS   1956

© OXFORD UNIVERSITY PRESS, Inc., 1956
PRINTED IN THE UNITED STATES OF AMERICA
LIBRARY OF CONGRESS CATALOG CARD NUMBER 56-10458

ILLUSTRATIONS

A PIERCING MARCH wind blew through the steep alleys of a little Spanish village in the province of Aragon one day in 1746. On that day a baby boy was born in one of the low stone cottages which clung to the barren hillside. The boy's name was Francisco Goya.

Francisco's father was poor, so when his son was very young he sent him to work in the fields. The sturdy little boy learned to endure icy winds and blistering summer sun. When Francisco was thirteen his father decided to move to the near-by city of Zaragossa, where he could find work and send his son to school.

At Father Joaquin's school in Zaragossa Francisco met a boy named Martin Zapater. Like Francisco, Martin loved to sing and hunt. Soon the boys were fast friends. On Sundays they went to bullfights. Sometimes the fearless Francisco would take part in a bullfight, while Martin looked on admiringly. In the afternoons, after they had finished their lessons, the boys would wander through the city streets. Often Francisco stopped to make sketches of the people he saw. When his father looked at his son's drawings of ladies in black veils and men in long cloaks and broad-brimmed hats, he decided that the boy should study art.

In the studio of a painter named Luzan, Francisco Goya was taught to copy Italian paintings. Although he preferred to draw pictures of Spanish people, he soon learned how to paint in the formal style of the Italians, and his teacher was pleased.

Each evening when the studio grew dark, Goya put his guitar under his arm and set out gaily with some of the other art students through the streets of Zaragossa. Sometimes he stopped to sing a serenade under a lady's balcony. Late into the night Goya and his friends sang and danced in the cafés of Zaragossa.

When Goya was seventeen the priest of the little village where Francisco was born asked him to paint an altarpiece of the Virgin appearing before Saint James. This was Goya's first big picture. The painting was crude, but when it was finished the parish priest placed it proudly above the altar of his little church.

APPARITION OF THE VIRGIN OF PILAR
Parish Church of Fuendetodos

Early one morning Francisco Goya was found lying in a dark alley in Zaragossa, a knife in his back. Friends carried him home, and in a few days his wound healed. This was not the first time the hot-tempered Goya had taken part in a street fight. His teacher, fearing for his pupil's life, urged Goya to leave Zaragossa. One dark night Goya left the city secretly, and with the money his father had given him he traveled to Madrid.

Goya was nineteen when he arrived in Madrid. Hoping to be admitted to Spain's finest art school, the Academy of San Fernando, he entered a painting competition, but his picture was not accepted. So he decided to join a group of bullfighters who were on their way to Italy.

Goya lived in Rome for two years, studying and copying Italian paintings. But more than once he took part in violent street fights, and again he feared for his life. Secretly Goya left Rome and returned to his home in Zaragossa.

At the studio of his teacher Luzan he met cold, formal Francisco Bayeu, member of the Academy of San Fernando and painter to the court of King Charles III. Bayeu was shocked by Goya's fiery manner, but he realized that the young artist had talent. One day he introduced Goya to his sister—golden-haired Josepha Bayeu. When she looked at Goya with her large quiet eyes, he decided he wanted her for his wife. Josepha was charmed by the impulsive young painter who did not wait long to ask for her hand. Soon Francisco and Josepha were married.

Although Francisco Bayeu did not approve of his new brother-in-law, he recognized his talent and asked Goya to help him in his work. So Goya took his gentle bride, whom he had nicknamed Pepa, to live in Madrid.

King Charles had just appointed Bayeu to paint pictures of Spanish life which later would be made into tapestry designs. Immediately happy scenes of dances, games and picnics flashed into Goya's mind. He painted a group of men and women dancing on the banks of the Manzanares River in Madrid, while two men accompany the dancers on guitars.

BALL OF SAN ANTONIO DE LA FLORIDA
(Tapestry Cartoon)
Prado, Madrid

In three years Goya painted thirty tapestry pictures, which told happy stories of Spanish life. He pictured gallant gentlemen and their ladies picnicking on the riverbank or playing blindman's buff. He painted a group of young men walking on stilts, and elegant ladies promenading with sunshades.

One of the prettiest pictures shows some grape pickers resting on a stone wall, their baskets filled with fruit. In the foreground stands a little boy who tries to snatch a cluster of grapes from a man who is sharing it with his lady.

Goya loved children. Over and over they appear in his pictures. He painted groups of children playing with bright-colored balloons, boys climbing trees, and a little boy riding on a black ram.

At the time Goya was working on his tapestry paintings his first son was born. But the baby was sickly and lived only a short while. Goya was heart-broken. In vain the gentle Pepa tried to comfort him.

Then Goya fell sick. For days he was too weak to leave his house to work on the tapestry paintings; so he set to work copying pictures of the Spanish painter Velasquez, which later he made into etchings. Goya admired the great artist who, one hundred years before, had painted scenes of Spanish life. Goya's etchings were crude, but when they were finished he sent them as a present to the king.

A few weeks later a royal messenger brought good news to the Goya home. King Charles III wanted the painter to visit him at his court. Goya had been waiting for this moment ever since he had arrived in Madrid.

Pepa rushed to get out Goya's best silk waistcoat and lace-trimmed blouse, while he put on his long white stockings and dress shoes. Then Goya kissed his wife good-by and hurried to the palace.

THE VINTAGE
(Tapestry Cartoon)
Prado, Madrid

Up the marble staircase of the king's palace strode stocky Francisco Goya. King Charles, his son, and daughter-in-law waited for him at the head of the stairs. Humbly Goya kissed the hand of the lean-faced king, and moved on to the king's son, tall, robust Prince Charles, and his ugly wife, Princess Maria Luisa. Goya answered modestly when the royal family praised his paintings.

When he returned home he sat down and wrote a long letter to his friend Martin in Zaragossa.

"If I had the time," he said, "I would tell you how I was honored by the king, the prince and the princess. I was able to kiss their hands—never have I experienced so much happiness. . . . Thanks be to God, I was not deserving of so much honor. Nor my works either."

Goya was thirty-three years old when he was received at the court of King Charles III. That same year he was asked to paint a portrait of the king dressed as a hunter. Although the portrait was not flattering, the king was pleased for it was a perfect likeness.

The king's shrewd, droopy face is framed by a three-cornered hat. He rests his left hand on a gun. At his feet lies a dog wearing a large collar on which is engraved the king's name.

Other painters at the Spanish court became jealous of Goya's popularity, and the young artist realized that this was a sign of success. He was confident that now he would be elected to the Royal Academy of San Fernando, which had refused to admit him thirteen years before. He painted a picture of Christ on the cross in the cold stilted style of the Italians and sent it to the Academy.

One July day in 1780 Goya received word that he had been made a member of the Royal Academy of San Fernando. Not one judge had voted against him.

CHARLES III AS A HUNTER
Municipal Museum, Madrid

There was one court painter who was glad of Goya's success. This was Francisco Bayeu, who now realized how much his talented brother-in-law could help him in his work. When Bayeu was commissioned to decorate a new marble chapel in Zaragossa, he asked Goya to design pictures for the ceiling.

Goya wrote happily to his friend Martin. Soon he would be seeing him in Zaragossa, he said. "For my house, I don't need much in the way of belongings," he wrote, "for I think that with a print of our Lady of Pilar, a table, five chairs, a stove, a cask, a guitar, a spit and a lamp, everything else is unnecessary."

In the fall of 1780 Goya, Pepa and their baby son arrived in Zaragossa.

"Thank God, a very healthy boy," Goya had said when the baby was born. His name was Francisco Javier.

Goya began immediately to paint huge pictures on the dome of the chapel of the Virgin of Pilar. He worked with furious energy, refusing to follow Bayeu's directions. In three months he had finished a painting of the Virgin on a bank of clouds, surrounded by cherubs and saints. Then he made sketches for the spaces under the dome.

Bayeu, annoyed that Goya had stubbornly ignored his orders, told the church committee that he did not approve of his brother-in-law's drawings. The committee agreed that the figures were not properly clothed, and asked him to draw a new set of sketches.

Bursting with rage, Goya wrote a long letter to the committee, accusing Bayeu of jealousy.

"Don Francisco Bayeu," he wrote, "feared the success of the signer of these lines, a success already obtained at court."

But Goya was finally persuaded to make a new set of drawings; and, sulkily following Bayeu's orders, he painted uninspired pictures on the chapel walls.

When the pictures were finished, the members of the committee sent a gleaming gold medal to the artist's wife, because, they explained, Josepha was the sister of Bayeu. But Goya received no decoration.

"When I think of those moments I spent in Zaragossa," Goya wrote later from Madrid, "my painting burns me alive."

14

VIRGIN APPEARING IN CLOUDS
Church of Our Lady of Pilar, Zaragossa

"I was very much crushed," wrote Goya, remembering the shame of Zaragossa, "but it has pleased God to comfort me." For soon after Goya returned to Madrid, the king commissioned him to paint a huge picture for his favorite church.

For three years Goya worked on the painting for the church of San Francisco el Grande, and when it was finished, he wrote to Martin: "It is certain I've had good fortune in the opinion of the authorities and the whole public."

Even greater fortune came to Goya that year of 1783. He was invited to visit at the country palace of one of the royal princes.

With astonishing speed he painted portraits of the prince, the princess and their children. In the afternoons the prince took the painter hunting, for Goya was an expert huntsman. When he left, the prince paid him handsomely and gave him a dress of gold and silver to take to Pepa.

"These princes, they are angels!" exclaimed Goya.

Orders poured in to Goya's studio. Generals, cabinet ministers and counts wanted their portraits painted. The brilliant Duchess of Osuna invited Goya to her country home. There he painted pictures of the duchess, her husband and their four children.

The Duchess of Osuna was called "the most distinguished woman of Madrid." She was a fearless horse-woman and a lover of bullfights. She organized concerts and plays and gave lectures on economics. She was also one of Europe's best-dressed women.

Goya painted her wearing a lace-trimmed hat decorated with ribbons and plumes. Her thick hair is brushed away from her long thin face. Her eyebrows are arched haughtily over cold, calm eyes.

Goya visited the Osuna family often. He painted pictures on the white and gold walls of their stately home, and decorated the inside of their private chapel. The duchess paid him well for his work.

"I am as contented as the happiest man on earth," Goya wrote to Martin.

THE DUCHESS OF OSUNA
Private Collection, Madrid

Francisco and Josepha moved into a fine new house over-looking the Manzanares River. Goya bought a shiny, gilded two-wheel carriage, but the first day he drove it through the streets of Madrid the carriage turned over and Goya was thrown into a ditch. When he tried to stand up he found that his leg was broken. The break healed quickly, however, and soon he was hard at work again.

"I have arranged a very agreeable life for myself," wrote Goya. "I no longer wait around in ante-rooms; the man who wants something of me comes to me to seek it."

But sadness came often to the Goya home. In ten years Francisco and Pepa had had five children, but only one had lived. Pepa was worn out with worry.

"My wife is ill, the child is worse, and even the servant has been stricken with fever," Goya wrote one spring day in 1787.

Soon after this Goya painted a portrait of the faithful Pepa. A thin scarf is folded demurely around her shoulders and large gray gloves cover her hands. Her red-gold hair has become dull and her large eyes are sad. Her thin lips are pressed tightly together, as if Josepha Goya had decided to accept her suffering quietly.

JOSEPHA GOYA
Prado, Madrid

Goya was a devoted father, who adored children. Because of his deep affection for all children, he loved to paint their portraits.

The little dark-haired prince Don Manuel Osorio was only four years old when Goya painted him. He is dressed in a suit of flaming red with a broad lace collar and a white sash. On the floor beside him is a cage filled with bright-colored birds, while on the other side three cats stare with gleaming eyes at the pet magpie which the little prince holds by a string. Goya signed his name on the piece of paper which the bird holds in his beak.

"I've become old with many wrinkles," Goya wrote to Martin at the time he was painting Don Manuel's portrait. "I am feeling my forty-one years very much." But Goya's portrait of the handsome four-year-old prince is one of the most charming pictures that has ever been painted of a little child.

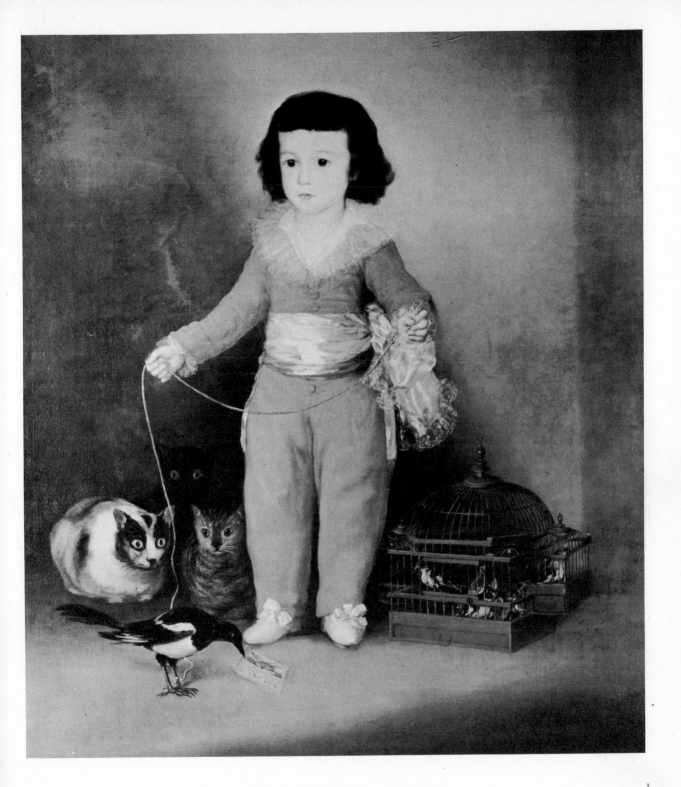

DON MANUEL OSORIO
Metropolitan Museum of Art, New York

"Martin, I am now a painter to the king!" wrote Goya exultantly in the spring of 1789. "I have taken the oath . . . with much pomp and ceremony."

Some months before, old King Charles had died. His son, slow, hulking Prince Charles, became king and named Don Francisco de Goya a painter to his court. Goya was overjoyed.

Childlike Charles IV was not interested in affairs of state. He preferred to go hunting every day, while his ministers took charge of the government. He loved to pose for his new court painter, who entertained him with stories about hunting. Because he liked to paint pictures himself, he marvelled that Goya could finish a brilliant portrait in a few hours. Portrait after portrait Goya painted of the king—once dressed in the costume of a hunter, but more often in royal dress.

In one portrait Charles IV wears a dark-blue coat bordered with jewels. Across his chest runs a broad ribbon to which is pinned a handsome jewelled cross. Behind him is a crown resting on an ermine cloak.

Although the king was about Goya's age, he looked many years older. Goya painted him as he saw him, with drooping nose, heavy chin and round eyes. Each portrait was a perfect likeness, and the genial king was delighted with every picture.

CHARLES IV
Prado, Madrid

Queen Maria Luisa, wife of Charles IV, was as disagreeable as she was ugly. She cared little for her slow-witted husband, whom she had been forced to marry when she was a girl of fifteen. She became enamoured of one of the palace guards, tall, stolid Manuel Godoy. Hoping to gain a place for himself in the king's court, Godoy returned the queen's affection. Maria Luisa showered him with honors. First she made him a colonel, then she asked the king to give him the title of duke. Charles granted her requests, too good-natured to suspect his deceitful wife and the scheming Godoy.

Arrayed in glittering finery, the vain queen loved to pose for the popular court painter. Skillfully Goya painted her gowns of gleaming satin, her sparkling jewels and huge hats of rippling lace. Mercilessly he painted her beady eyes, beaked nose and large thin-lipped mouth. Although the fearless artist showed the ugly queen exactly as she was, Maria Luisa was pleased, because the court's most popular artist had painted a perfect likeness. As soon as one picture was finished, she ordered Goya to paint another.

QUEEN MARIA LUISA
Royal Academy of History, Madrid

"Setting all jokes aside, long-nosed Martin," Goya wrote from Madrid, "I am going to have the canvas prepared for your portrait, for I shall not rest in peace until I have painted it."

For years Martin had been begging his artist friend to paint his portrait, but Goya could not take time from his work in Madrid.

"The picture, I will do it," Goya wrote at last. Commissions from Spanish nobles would have to wait while Goya took a short trip to Zaragossa. "But believe me," he wrote to Martin, "only your friendship would make me do it."

"Martin, companion of my soul," Goya once called his loyal friend. For thirty years the quiet, kindly Martin had listened patiently to Goya's outbursts of rage, and rejoiced with him in his moments of triumph. Letter after letter Goya wrote to Martin, telling him of his worries and his joys. Sometimes he decorated his letters with sketches. When Martin's father died, Goya promised to paint "a very beautiful Virgin" for his friend. When Goya was penniless Martin loaned him money.

But Goya was not penniless when he came to Zaragossa to paint Martin's portrait. He was a successful painter to the king, and very busy. He did not want Martin to forget that he had left important commissions in Madrid in order to paint his friend's portrait.

So when the picture of long-nosed Martin was finished he wrote on the piece of paper which his genial friend holds in his hand: "My friend Martin Zapater, by dint of hard work, your portrait has been painted by Goya, 1790."

MARTIN ZAPATER
Durand-Ruel, Paris

The Duchess of Alba was twenty-nine years old when Goya met her at the king's court. She was wealthy, charming and startlingly beautiful.

Goya, who loved to paint beautiful women, was fascinated by the lovely duchess, and she was charmed by the witty court painter who dared to paint people as he saw them. Goya was elated when the duchess asked him to paint her portrait.

Many times the duchess visited Goya's studio. Goya told Martin of how one day, while he was painting a picture, the impulsive duchess burst into his workroom and asked him to paint pictures on her face.

"Of course she obtained what she desired," Goya wrote. "I must say I like this better than painting on canvas."

The duchess invited Goya to visit her at her country palace; there he painted her portrait again. One bitter day he caught cold, and for weeks he lay desperately ill. Stubbornly the vigorous Goya fought for his life, until at last he was able to move and talk; but he could hear nothing. His illness had made him completely deaf.

Plunged in a world of silence, Goya filled notebook after notebook with sketches of the enchanting duchess. In one drawing she tears her hair despairingly, because her little dog has died; in another, she holds a little Negro girl on her lap, and in still another she flirts over her fan with a dashing admirer.

Goya looked haggard and old when he returned to Madrid. He was totally deaf, but was still able to paint portraits at dizzying speed. When the Duchess of Alba returned from her country home, Goya painted her again, wearing a black dress with a bright-red sash. On her head is a black lace veil, called a mantilla.

The duchess stands proudly pointing to the ground, on which is traced Goya's name. Two big rings decorate her hand. On one is written "Goya," and on the other "Alba."

THE DUCHESS OF ALBA
Hispanic Society of America, New York

"I am sometimes so disturbed that I can no longer endure myself," wrote Goya to his friend Martin.

Cut off from conversation with people, Goya studied their expressions and gestures. The people of the court appeared to him foolish and insincere. Even the beautiful Duchess of Alba seemed frivolous and fickle. Lonely Goya began to express these thoughts in drawings, which ridiculed the foolishness of man.

"No one knows himself," Goya wrote under a drawing of two masked people talking to each other. He drew a picture of a donkey having his portrait painted by a monkey. Perhaps the donkey is supposed to be the foolish king. Another picture shows a hideous hag trying on a hat before a group of admiring gentlemen. The hag looks very much like the ugly queen.

Maybe Goya was thinking of the queen's favorite, Godoy, who had just been made a duke, when he drew a long-eared donkey looking at a picture book of ancestors, all of whom are donkeys. "As far back as his grandfather," Goya wrote under the picture.

These were some of the thoughts which Goya illustrated. He etched his strange drawings on copper plates, so that they could be printed many times. In a letter to a friend Goya described his drawings as pictures of "caprice and invention"; so when the set of etchings was printed he called it the *Caprichos*.

AS FAR BACK AS HIS GRANDFATHER
(from the *Caprichos*)
Hispanic Society of America, New York

Goya made eighty *Capricho* etchings. He pictured ignorant humans beset by terrifying monsters which were supposed to be the evil forces in the world. Perhaps the hideous witches, dwarfs and elves in Goya's etchings were the creatures which had haunted his nightmares at the time of his sickness.

One etching shows Goya asleep at his desk, his head buried in his arms, while eerie screech owls, bats and vultures fly around him. A huge cat with gleaming eyes sits at his feet.

"Dreams of reason produce monsters," Goya wrote under the picture.

One winter day in 1799 Goya's *Caprichos* were displayed in a small shop in Madrid; but a few days later Goya removed his etchings from the shop.

"I wish to make them a gift to the king, my master, for his collection," wrote Goya. Perhaps the artist feared the wrath of the people whom he had ridiculed; but he knew that the kindly king would not be able to understand the meaning of his witty drawings.

Goya requested only one favor when he presented his eighty brilliant etchings to King Charles. He asked that his son, Javier, be given money to study art. Gladly the king granted Goya's request.

DREAMS OF REASON PRODUCE MONSTERS
(from the *Caprichos*)
Hispanic Society of America, New York

Javier was the only one of Goya's and Josepha's twenty children who lived to grow up. Goya had once described his son as "the loveliest thing to be seen in Madrid."

When Javier was a young man his adoring father painted his portrait, fashionably dressed in a long-tailed coat and tight britches. One hand is tucked into his richly embroidered vest and the other hand holds a hat and a cane. The wooly toy dog at his feet is like the ones which were popular at the Spanish court. This elegant young man, who received a fine income from the king, was about to marry the daughter of a wealthy gentleman from Zaragossa. He was also the son of Spain's most celebrated painter, and so, with the careless confidence of a man of the world, Javier posed for his proud father.

JAVIER GOYA
Collection of Comtesse de Noailles, Paris

Every morning during the glowing autumn of 1798 one of the king's coaches called at Goya's home to drive him into the country to the chapel of San Antonio de la Florida. The little church, not far from the king's country palace, was used by the royal family and their friends. King Charles had commissioned his favorite painter to decorate the chapel ceiling. As the royal coach wound its way along the shady banks of the Menzenares River, Goya peered eagerly from the window. He saw groups of children at play, women in bright costumes, stalwart peasants and beggars in rags. These were the people Goya planned to paint on the ceiling of the little chapel.

He climbed onto the scaffolding under the dome and painted at furious speed. Using sponges tied to long sticks, he washed on the paint in the wide spaces he wished to cover quickly. In four months he filled the chapel ceiling with a throng of lively people. Behind a railing which Goya painted around the base of the dome is a pushing jostling throng which has come to watch Saint Anthony bring a dead man to life. The saint stands above the crowd, leaning forward tensely, his hand raised in blessing as he performs the miracle. Winged angels with trumpets and blond cherubs dressed in costumes of Goya's day fill the spaces below the dome. The pretty angels and plump pink-and-white cherubs look like dancers in a ballet, and the men, women and children look like real people from the streets of Madrid who have rushed to see an exciting spectacle.

The joyous scene, which is painted in beautiful tones of rose, yellow, blue and green, is bathed in a silver light. The artist who had drawn the dark nightmares of the *Caprichos* had suddenly emerged into a gay and brilliant world.

The little church of San Antonio de la Florida was opened in the fall of 1799, and the people of Madrid came to marvel at the luminous paintings which covered the chapel ceiling. A few weeks later Don Francisco de Goya was appointed first painter to the court of Spain.

THE MIRACLE OF SAINT ANTHONY
Church of San Antonio de la Florida, Madrid

The spring of 1800 was a busy one for the court's first painter. In the fine coach provided by the king, Goya traveled between Madrid and King Charles' favorite summer palace. He painted many portraits in the rooms overlooking the magnificent royal gardens.

The beak-nosed queen, imitating the beautiful Duchess of Alba, asked to have her portrait painted wearing the costume of the Spanish people. Goya painted her again, riding side-saddle on the fine horse which Manuel Godoy had given her.

"They say it is even a better likeness than the one in a mantilla," wrote Maria Luisa to Godoy.

Then Goya painted a picture of the fat king on horseback, and Charles was delighted.

At the king's summer palace Goya made life-size sketches of every one of the thirteen members of the royal family, for Charles had asked him to paint a picture of his whole family together.

One after the other, Goya placed on a huge canvas the people he had sketched so truthfully. In the middle stands the forbidding queen, resplendent in a white dress spangled with gold and silver. In her hair is a great jewelled arrow. On her left is her youngest son, whom she holds by the hand, and her right arm rests protectingly on the shoulder of her daughter. The heavy, dull king stands in the foreground, dressed in brown velvet, his bulging chest covered with sparkling medals. The stunted figure of the king's son Ferdinand stands at the left of the picture. The lady next to him is his fiancée, who had not yet arrived at the Spanish court. Having no model to draw from, Goya turned her face away from the picture. The old lady with the long nose and popping eyes who stands between the prince and the princess is the king's sister.

Behind the glittering array of sparkling jewels, shimmering silks and rich velvets stands Goya at his easel. Dressed in a dark coat, he can scarcely be seen in the dim left corner. Solemnly he looks over the heads of the royal family. So Goya humbly presents himself as first painter to the court of King Charles.

FAMILY OF CHARLES IV
Prado, Madrid

Goya does not look humble in the etching he made of himself wearing a tall black hat. He looks sullenly from under his bushy eyebrows and his lower lip is thrust forward arrogantly. His expression is confident and bold, for Goya at fifty-seven was Spain's most successful painter.

He and Josepha now lived in a fine villa overlooking the Manzanares River. His only son was married to the daughter of a wealthy man, and Francisco Goya knew that he was very popular at the court of Spain.

Even the queen's favorite, Godoy, now prime minister, liked Goya and invited him to his palace. Although Goya had ridiculed Godoy in his *Caprichos*, he was flattered by the prime minister's attentions. He wrote Martin about his visit. Godoy took him riding in his carriage, he said.

"He permitted me to wear my cloak at dinner, because it was very cold," Goya wrote. "He learned to speak with his hands and would stop eating in order to converse with me."

King Charles was so fond of his favorite court painter that he tried in every way to please him. In a letter to Martin, Goya told of how one day the stupid king, forgetting that the artist was deaf, decided to entertain his court painter by playing to him on the violin. The simple king did not play well, but deaf Goya heard nothing.

Even when Goya ignored the formalities of the court, Charles welcomed his favorite painter cordially. One day when the members of the court were in mourning dress, Goya appeared in white knee britches and long white stockings. The guards refused to admit him unless he changed his costume. The painter turned on his heel and disappeared; but in a few minutes he returned. His long white stockings were covered with cartoons of the king's guards. Boldly he marched by the astonished guards into the palace. So amused was the king when he saw Goya's clever drawings that he received his court painter more cordially than ever.

SELF PORTRAIT
(from the *Caprichos*)
Hispanic Society of America, New York

Crafty Manuel Godoy, Prime Minister of Spain and Commander-in-Chief of the army, was a cruel dictator who cared little for the Spanish people. He plunged his country into a war against France, and when the war went badly for Spain, Godoy was forced to sign a peace treaty which gave a big slice of Spanish land to France. The simple king, however, urged on by the queen, honored his prime minister by giving him the impressive title of the "Prince of Peace."

Wearing the glittering uniform of generalissimo of the army, the "Prince of Peace" sat while Goya painted his portrait. His flabby figure is sprawled on a low sofa. A lieutenant stands behind him, ready to receive the orders which Godoy holds in his hand. Officers and horses are waiting in the background.

The "Prince of Peace" appears confident of his power as he leans lazily against the arm of the sofa, though at this time the mighty armies of Napoleon were sweeping across Europe. Too late Godoy realized that he was powerless to defend Spain against a French invasion. In the spring of 1808 the soldiers of the Emperor Napoleon began to march across the mountains into Spain.

MANUEL GODOY—PRINCE OF PEACE
Academy of San Fernando, Madrid

The troops of Napoleon were greeted with shouts of joy when they marched into the mountain villages of Spain in the spring of 1808. The Spanish people believed that the French had come to liberate them from the cruel and powerful Godoy. On toward Madrid marched the army of the emperor. Trembling, the fat Godoy hid in his palace, while a furious mob surrounded his home and finally dragged him from his attic room.

In terror the muddled king gave over his throne to his son Ferdinand, bitter enemy of Godoy. Godoy was thrown into prison and Charles and his ugly queen fled to their country palace. A few days later the French army walked into Madrid.

One sunny day in May a crowd gathered around the royal palace in Madrid. The people had come to see the youngest children of King Charles depart. French soldiers guarded the coaches, which were waiting at the palace gates. Then someone in the crowd said he heard the king's youngest son crying because he did not want to leave the palace. A woman shrieked that the little boy was being kidnaped by Napoleon. Suddenly the crowd became angry, because the French were taking away their little prince. Workmen with knives surrounded the coach, cut the harness and led the horses away. French cannon fired into the mob, but the angry people could not be put down. Laborers, tradesmen, peasants, armed with whatever weapons they could find, surged into the narrow streets of Madrid. The emperor's soldiers fired at them mercilessly. Into one of the public squares thundered a company of Napoleon's Egyptian horsemen. Their curved swords flashed in the sun as they fell upon the crowd. With sticks and daggers the Spaniards fought back ferociously. Some attacked the riders with their bare hands.

This is what Goya saw that day in Madrid, and in quick angry strokes he sketched the scene. From his sketches Goya painted a violent picture which is called "El Dos de Mayo," or "The Second of May," for it was on that day that the people of Madrid rose up and fought the French invaders.

EL DOS DE MAYO
Prado, Madrid

Only a few people were still fighting in the streets of Madrid when the sun went down on the second of May. But in every part of the city Spaniards who were found with knives or daggers were arrested and shot by the French soldiers. All that night and into the next morning the guns of the French firing squad could be heard in Madrid.

From the window of his home Goya could see the flash of gunfire on a near-by hillside. For a few minutes the moon shone between the clouds and Goya saw the backs of the French firing squad. A dark row of soldiers, feet planted firmly, shoulders thrust forward, aimed their guns at a man in a white shirt. The prisoner was kneeling, arms thrust upward, eyes flashing, boldly challenging the guns which were about to shoot him. The bodies of the dead lay on the ground in front of him. Beside him knelt a man, hands clasped, imploring mercy. More prisoners staggered up the hill in the dim background. One man in terror was biting his clenched fist, another plunged his face in his hands, shielding his eyes from the brutal scene of slaughter.

Goya never forgot the horror of that night. The sight of the bold Spaniard in a white shirt shrieking defiance in the face of ruthless gunfire, remained a vivid picture in his mind. Six years later he told the story of that night of slaughter in his stirring masterpiece called "The Executions of the Third of May."

THE EXECUTIONS OF THE THIRD OF MAY
Prado, Madrid

As the news of that dreadful third of May spread to every city and village in Spain, angry people rose up against the invading armies. When Napoleon sent his brother Joseph to take over the throne of Spain, King Ferdinand fled from Madrid. For four long years the Spaniards fought to free their country from the French invader. Three times Joseph Bonaparte entered Madrid under the protection of the French army, and three times he was forced to flee.

During these black years Goya saw death and destruction in his country. French soldiers robbed churches, peasants were bayonetted, houses destroyed and children died of hunger. Burning with hatred and overwhelmed with pity, Goya drew pictures which told of the savage cruelty of war. The set of etchings which he made from his drawings is called the *Disasters of War*.

The first of these great etchings shows a man on his knees, arms thrown up in despair, defenseless against the disaster which is about to strike him.

"Sad premonition of things to come," wrote Goya under this tragic picture.

SAD PREMONITION OF THINGS TO COME
(from the *Disasters of War*)
Hispanic Society of America, New York

During one whole summer the French bombarded the town of Zaragossa. When at last Napoleon's soldiers forced their way into the city, men, women and children fell upon the troops with sticks and stones and pieces of broken glass, until the enemy retreated.

Stirred by the news of the victory, Goya traveled from Madrid to look at the ruins of the town where he had lived as a young man. With his friend Martin, he walked through the devastated streets. He was deeply moved by what he saw and could not turn away, because, as he wrote, "Of the great interest I have in the glory of my fatherland."

All that autumn Goya stayed in Zaragossa, drawing pictures of the terrible ruins. He was told the thrilling tale of the beautiful young girl who had become the heroine of Zaragossa.

This brave young girl was standing near the Spanish cannon one day when the French were firing relentlessly at the city. One after the other she saw the Spaniards fall under the enemy fire, until there was no one left to man the guns. Plunging forward over the dead bodies, she snatched a smoking fuse from the hand of a dying man and fired off one of the cannon. The sound of the shot brought courage to the people of Zaragossa. More Spaniards rushed to man the silent guns. So fierce was the firing that day that the French finally gave up the attack. When the sun went down the heroic girl, riding on the cannon she had fired, returned in triumph to Zaragossa.

One of the finest of Goya's *Disasters of War* etchings shows this brave, beautiful girl as she touches the smoking fuse to the cannon.

"What courage" was Goya's title for this picture.

WHAT COURAGE
(from the *Disasters of War*)
Hispanic Society of America, New York

For three long years the Spaniards had endured the miseries of war. A terrible famine struck Madrid the winter of 1811, and during that hungry winter Josepha Goya died.

The lonely Goya lived on in his big house, making etchings of the *Disasters of War*. During the short reigns of Joseph Bonaparte, he was asked to paint portraits of French generals. He even painted a picture of King Joseph. The "Intruder King," as he was called by the people of Madrid, sent Goya a gold medal hung on a purple ribbon. The Spaniards scornfully called the decoration the "Order of the Eggplant." Goya refused to wear it.

In the spring of 1812 the people of Madrid learned that the Duke of Wellington had landed in Portugal, and was leading his red-coated British troops across the border into Spain. Wild with joy, the Spaniards welcomed the man who would liberate them from the French. On toward the Spanish capital marched the duke. Joseph asked his brother for help, but Napoleon had no more troops to send to Spain. In terror the "Intruder King" fled Madrid for the last time.

One blazing August day the church bells of Madrid pealed exultantly as a slim, severe figure in a gray coat and cocked hat led his scarlet-coated troops into the city. From every window flowers showered down on the great general who had defeated the armies of Napoleon. Women rushed to kiss his sword and his boots. Silently the Duke of Wellington rode on.

This was the man, hooked-nosed, trim and austere, whom Goya saw that day in Madrid. Three times he painted the great duke's portrait.

THE DUKE OF WELLINGTON
Courtesy of Mrs. P. H. B. Frelinghuysen

Photograph courtesy of the Metropolitan Museum of Art

As the last soldiers of Napoleon retreated across the mountains into France, Ferdinand VII, son of Charles IV, returned to Madrid.

With passionate loyalty the Spaniards had fought to bring Ferdinand back to the throne of Spain; but soon they realized that their king was a cruel tyrant, who cared little for the liberty of his people.

The contempt which Goya felt for Ferdinand is expressed in every portrait he painted of the king. At dizzying speed the sixty-eight-year-old artist, once more painter to the court, turned out pictures of Ferdinand. He painted one huge portrait in three hours. Sometimes the king was dressed in royal robes or brilliant uniforms. In one picture he sits like a puppet astride a prancing horse.

Goya showed the new king exactly as he was. In every portrait the dark eyes of Ferdinand are full of hatred, and his sneering mouth is cruel.

FERDINAND VII
Academy of San Fernando, Madrid

Whenever he was able Goya escaped from the court of the hated Ferdinand to his home, which people had named the "Deaf Man's Villa." There he worked on his etchings of the *Disasters of War.* The horrors of the long war with France still lived vividly in his memory; and it was at this time that he painted his two violent pictures "El Dos de Mayo" and "The Executions of the Third of May."

Goya remembered happier times too. He thought of the days in Zaragossa when he sat under the blazing sun with his friend Martin and watched exciting bullfights. He remembered, too the times he had fought in the ring. "Francisco of the bulls" he had once signed himself in a letter to a friend.

In vigorous drawings Goya started to describe the art of bull-fighting, which he understood so well. While he was still working on the *Disasters of War,* he began a series of etchings which told the history of bullfighting in Spain. He showed how, hundreds of years before, the peasants had fought the bull in the open field. He told how darts, or *banderillas,* were first used, and then how it became fashionable for noblemen to fight the bull in an enclosed ring.

One etching shows the great Emperor Charles V, who ruled Spain two hundred years before Goya's day, fighting the bull on horseback. The bearded emperor, dressed in splendid military uniform with armoured leg guards and plumed hat, leans forward on his galloping steed and skillfully plunges his lance into the neck of the charging bull.

CHARLES V AND BULL IN THE PLAZA VALLADOLID
(from *La Tauromaquia*)
Hispanic Society of America, New York

Vividly Goya pictured the amazing skill of famous bullfighters of his day.

One etching shows a well-known bullfighter named Juanito Apinari pole-vaulting gracefully over the back of a charging bull.

In the background tense spectators are watching the exciting act. The shady section behind the barrier is filled with people, while in the sunny section a small group is huddled under an umbrella.

"The lightness and dexterity of Juanito Apinari" is the name Goya gave to the etching he made of this brilliant feat of bravery.

THE LIGHTNESS AND DEXTERITY
OF JUANITO APINARI
(from *La Tauromaquia*)
Hispanic Society of America, New York

The "Deaf Man's Villa" stood on a shady hillside. In the early morning Goya liked to walk about the garden under the cool shade of the green trees and watch the mist rising from the river below. When the sun grew hot, the tall, high-ceilinged house was a peaceful retreat.

Goya was not alone in his villa, for his cousin, a domineering woman, had come to keep house for him after the death of the faithful Josepha. With her came her baby daughter, Rosario, whom Goya loved as if she were his own child.

But deaf Goya lived in a world apart. His mind was filled with strange thoughts, and these thoughts he painted on the dining-room walls of his home. "The Black Paintings," people called Goya's dark pictures of monstrous giants and hollow-eyed witches. He decorated the walls of his study too. With broad, violent strokes he brought to life fantastic dreams of flying men, desolate landscapes and cities built on rocky peaks.

It was at this time that Goya painted his own portrait, head tilted to one side as he looked at himself in the mirror. His dark eyes were sad, his mouth unsmiling. The face of the sixty-nine-year-old Goya was grave, but it had not lost its rugged vigor.

SELF PORTRAIT
Smith College Museum of Art, Northampton, Mass.

While Goya worked on his "Black Paintings," little Rosario trotted happily around the big house. Sometimes she tip-toed into the dining room and watched fascinated as Goya painted strange pictures on the white walls. Goya loved to have her near him. His happiest moments were those he spent with children, and when he painted them the bitter thoughts which troubled him seemed to vanish.

He painted charming portraits of his grandson Mariano, son of Goya's adored Javier. When the little boy was six years old, he posed for his grandfather, dressed in a velvet suit and a tall hat. Sheets of music are propped up beside him. Serious little Mariano seems to be listening intently, as if he was beating time with the folded paper which he holds in his right hand.

MARIANO GOYA

Collection Duke of Alburquerque, Madrid

Goya fell seriously ill in the autumn of 1819. All through that winter he fought his sickness stubbornly, and when spring came he was back at work once more. He began to put on paper the nightmares of his illness, just as he had thirty-five years before when he drew the *Caprichos*. These frightening pictures from which Goya made a set of etchings told of man's foolishness, and he called them the *Disparates,* or *Stupidities.*

Goya wrote no notes under the etchings to explain the meaning of his terrifying pictures. Many of them are hard to understand, but all of them tell a bitter story.

One picture shows a group of people huddled on the end of a dead branch, which is about to fall. Perhaps the branch is a symbol of man's uncertain life, which can be cut off suddenly.

"The stupidity of fright" is the name Goya gave to one of the *Disparates*. A huge ghostlike figure pursues a group of terrified soldiers, who look ridiculously tiny in contrast to the scarecrow which towers over them. Perhaps Goya wanted to show in this picture the foolishness of people who are frightened by imaginary fears.

THE STUPIDITY OF FRIGHT
(from the *Disparates*)
Hispanic Society of America, New York

Many of Goya's friends went to live in France during the reign of the cruel Ferdinand; for the king who had promised freedom to Spain had brought only tyranny and bloodshed. Although Goya was still a painter to the king, he seldom visited the royal court. Fearing the ruthless dictatorship of Ferdinand, he decided to seek safety and freedom with his friends in France.

One day Goya received a letter from the court: "Our lord the King, yielding to the request of the painter Don Francisco Goya, has been pleased to accord him His Majesty's royal license to go to take the mineral waters . . . in France, in order to assuage his rheumatism."

Goya was nearly eighty years old when he set out alone on a long and tiring trip across the mountains to France.

"Goya has indeed arrived," wrote one of his friends from the city of Bordeaux, "enfeebled, not knowing a word of French . . . nevertheless very well satisfied and very eager to see the world."

Three days later Goya was on his way to Paris. There he visited friends and painted portraits. But when winter came he returned to sunny Bordeaux.

He moved into a fine apartment with his cousin and the little Rosario, who had followed Goya to Bordeaux. He set to work with his usual vigor. Because his eyes had grown weak, he could no longer draw fine-lined etchings, but he learned to make a new kind of print called a lithograph. Using a big crayon, he drew on a flat stone which he propped on an easel. He worked with amazing speed, not even stopping to sharpen his crayon. He made magnificent drawings of bullfights, and from these drawings a set of lithographs was printed. The set was called *The Bulls of Bordeaux.*

The first print shows a famous American bullfighter, spear in hand, riding on the back of a charging bull.

But *The Bulls of Bordeaux* did not sell, and Goya feared that his salary as court painter would be cut off if he remained in France. So early in the summer of 1826 the aged Goya set off alone by stagecoach over steep and perilous roads. Two weeks later he arrived in Madrid.

THE FAMOUS AMERICAN MATADOR
MARIANO CEBALLOS
(from *The Bulls of Bordeaux*)
National Gallery of Art, Washington, D. C.

Rosenwald Collection

King Ferdinand received Goya at his court and assured the artist that his salary as court painter would continue for the rest of his life. But soon Goya realized that he could not be happy in Madrid. Although he loved Spain, he could not endure the brutal dictatorship of Ferdinand, and he missed his friends in Bordeaux.

Before he left Madrid, he drove out to the little church of San Antonio de la Florida to take a last look at the spirited figures he had painted on the dome. He arranged to leave the "Deaf Man's Villa" to his son, Javier. Then one summer day he set off once more for France.

"He is busy sketching," wrote a friend from Bordeaux. "Goes out walking, eats and takes his after-dinner nap. It seems to me that peace reigns."

Wearing a broad-brimmed hat, Goya strolled about the streets of the city, sketching the people he saw. A blind beggar holding out his hat attracted his attention. He drew the bent figure leaning on a cane, and the fat dog which the beggar held by a string.

One spring day in 1828 Goya received the happy news that Mariano and his mother were on their way to Bordeaux.

"I cannot tell you anything more," Goya wrote to Javier. "So much joy has made me a little ill, and I am in bed. Please God you may come to join them, so my happiness may be complete."

A few days later Goya could not move or speak. Anxiously his cousin and Mariano watched over him. Then early one morning, before his adored Javier reached Bordeaux, Francisco Goya died.

"A most skilled painter" was the only inscription placed on Goya's gravestone in Bordeaux. Seventy years went by before the body of the great artist was taken back to Madrid. Today Francisco Goya lies buried in the little church of San Antonio de la Florida, under the bright dome on which he brought to life a throng of joyous angels and a lively crowd of people from the streets of Madrid.

BLIND BEGGAR
Collection Lazaro, Madrid